IN THE NEWS Need to Know

SilverTip

Deepfakes

by Ashley Kuehl

Consultant: Caitlin Krieck, Social Studies Teacher and Instructional Coach, The Lab School of Washington

BEARPORT PUBLISHING

Minneapolis, Minnesota

Credits

Cover and title page, © PintoArt/Shutterstock and © Vikks/Shutterstock; 5, © Eduard Figueres/iStock; 7, © Jose Miguel Sanchez/iStock; 9, © Prostock-studio/Adobe Stock; 11, © Daniel/Adobe Stock; 13, © PR Image Factory/Adobe Stock and © BazziBa/Adobe Stock and © Drobot Dean/Adobe Stock and © Drobot Dean/Adobe Stock; 15, © twinsterphoto/Adobe Stock and © deagreez/Adobe Stock; 17, © Digital Photo Professional/Adobe Stock; 19, © Pier Marco Tacca/Getty Images; 21, © Andrey Popov/Adobe Stock; 23, © Anna Moneymaker/Getty Images; 25, © Gorodenkoff /Adobe Stock; 27, © kali9/iStock; 28TL, © Public Domain/Wikimedia; 28ML, © Public Domain/Wikimedia; 28BL, © Public Domain/Wikimedia

Bearport Publishing Company Product Development Team

Publisher: Jen Jenson; Director of Product Development: Spencer Brinker; Managing Editor: Allison Juda; Editor: Cole Nelson; Associate Editor: Naomi Reich; Associate Editor: Tiana Tran; Art Director: Colin O'Dea; Designer: Kim Jones; Designer: Kayla Eggert; Product Development Specialist: Owen Hamlin

Statement on Usage of Generative Artificial Intelligence

Bearport Publishing remains committed to publishing high-quality nonfiction books. Therefore, we restrict the use of generative AI to ensure accuracy of all text and visual components pertaining to a book's subject. See BearportPublishing.com for details.

Quote Sources

Page 28: Joe Biden from "Remarks by President Biden and Vice President Harris on the Administration's Commitment to Advancing the Safe, Secure, and Trustworthy Development and Use of Artificial Intelligence," *whitehouse.gov*, October 30, 2023; María Elvira Salazar from "Salazar Introduces Legislation to Protect Victims of Deepfake Revenge Porn," *Salazar.house.gov*, July 10, 2024; Bill Gates from "Bill Gates Talks to CNET About AI, Misinformation and Climate Change," *CNET*, September 5, 2024

Library of Congress Cataloging-in-Publication Data is available at www.loc.gov or upon request from the publisher.

ISBN: 979-8-89232-765-7 (hardcover)
ISBN: 979-8-89232-940-8 (paperback)
ISBN: 979-8-89232-852-4 (ebook)

Copyright © 2025 Bearport Publishing Company. All rights reserved. No part of this publication may be reproduced in whole or in part, stored in any retrieval system, or transmitted in any form or by any means, electronic, mechanical, photocopying, recording, or otherwise, without written permission from the publisher.

For more information, write to Bearport Publishing, 5357 Penn Avenue South, Minneapolis, MN 55419.

Contents

That's Not Right! 4

Faking It 6

Making It Seem Real 10

Faces and Voices 14

Fake Events 16

How You Can Help 20

Laws, Rules, and Tools 22

What Happens Next? 26

Voices in the News 28

SilverTips for Success 29

Glossary 30

Read More 31

Learn More Online 31

Index .32

About the Author 32

That's Not Right!

Your friend sends you a video online. It shows two **celebrities** saying mean things about their fans. The people in the video look and sound like they always do. But these stars never said those things. The video is not real. It's a deepfake.

Some people make many deepfakes of one celebrity. They make social media accounts for the photos and videos. Sometimes, the accounts have huge followings. They trick many people into believing things that aren't true.

Faking It

Deepfakes are pieces of fake **content** that look or sound very real. This fake content is made using **artificial intelligence (AI)**. Some are images that have been made up or changed. Others are **audio** files. There are also faked videos.

Some people get fake calls that sound like a family member. It may seem like their loved ones are asking for money or are in trouble.

Deepfake phone calls try to trick or steal from people.

People have been making fake pictures and videos for a long time. But it was easier to know they were not real in the past. Faked photos were often blurry or had weird shadows. Voices sounded strange. Today's deepfakes look and sound very realistic. This can make them more dangerous.

In 1917, Elsie Wright made one of the first faked photos. It showed her cousin surrounded by fairies. The image even tricked the author of *Sherlock Holmes!*

Some faked images are easier to spot than others.

Making It Seem Real

People make deepfakes using a kind of AI called **deep learning**. This AI works by first being fed a lot of content. A computer program studies the **data**. It finds patterns and learns how to copy them. Then, another computer program called a **generator** makes new content based on this information.

A computer program needs to study many photos before making a deepfake image. This helps the computer find small details that make new content look real.

> Powerful computers are needed to make very realistic deepfakes.

Another part of the program checks the new content. It compares what has been made to real images or videos. Then, it sends **feedback** to the generator. It tells the generator what was good or bad. The generator tries again. This repeats until the program decides the content seems real.

Deepfakes aren't just used to trick people. Some online stores use them to show people wearing the stores' products. Customers can see what they may look like before they buy.

Faces and Voices

There are many kinds of deepfakes. In a face swap, one person's face is put on another person's body. Other deepfakes are videos that include both faked visuals and sounds. A person seems to be saying the words you hear.

Some people make fake content without AI. But it is usually easy to spot as not real. These bad fakes are called cheapfakes or shallow fakes.

It is hard to make face swaps look real without using AI.

Fake Events

Some deepfakes may be fun. But many cause problems. People can be tricked into thinking fake content is real. They could believe someone in a deepfake video said or did something hurtful. This can get people in these videos in trouble. They might lose their jobs.

In 2024, someone made a deepfake recording. It sounded like a school principal saying hurtful things. But the principal never said those things. Still, the recording spread. The principal was almost fired.

People have also made deepfakes of government leaders. In 2024, a fake **robocall** went to thousands of people. In the call, it sounded like then-President Joe Biden told people not to vote. But President Biden never made this message. It was a deepfake that sounded just like him.

In 2024, a deepfake video of Ukraine's president appeared online. It showed the president telling soldiers to give up fighting a war against Russia. Luckily, the soldiers knew it was fake.

Ukrainian President Volodymyr Zelenskyy

How You Can Help

There are ways we can all stop harmful deepfakes. Always make sure to **fact-check** content. Make sure a photo is real or a fact is true. Do this before you share anything online or with friends. If you discover fake content, don't share it with other people.

Certain clues can help you spot fake pictures. Does someone have too many fingers? Does their hair look strange? Are they doing things they don't usually do? The picture might be fake.

Laws, Rules, and Tools

Just knowing how to spot deepfakes may not be enough to keep people safe. Governments are taking action. They are making it illegal to make certain kinds of deepfakes. Some people who make hurtful deepfakes can be arrested. People can sue if their face or voice is used in a deepfake without asking.

In 2024, U.S. lawmakers introduced a law about deepfakes. It made it illegal to post or share fake images of people without asking them. Websites must take down these images.

In 2024, singer-songwriter twigs spoke to Congress about the dangers of deepfakes.

Some social media companies, news groups, and computer developers are helping, too. They are building tools to find fake content. These tools can remove deepfakes or make users prove who they are. This can help stop deepfakes from tricking people.

Some people make deepfake music. The music sounds like a certain artist made it. The person who made the deepfake can make money from it. But the real artist gets nothing.

What Happens Next?

Computer experts are making new ways to stop harmful deepfakes. Some people are using AI to spot fake images or videos. Artists are adding special marks to their work that stop people from using it for deepfakes. Technology can do amazing things. But we must be careful to use it safely.

Some schools teach about AI and deepfakes. Students learn how to tell if content is real. They learn what to do with fake or harmful content.

Voices in the News

People have many things to say about deepfakes. Some of their voices can be heard in the news.

Joe Biden
Former United States President

"Deepfakes use AI-generated audio and video to smear reputations, spread fake news, and commit fraud."

María Elvira Salazar
U.S. House Representative

"The alarming rise of deepfakes is threatening to destroy innocent individuals' and families' lives."

Bill Gates
Entrepreneur and Philanthropist

"With things like deepfakes, most of the time you're online you're going to want to be in an environment where the people are truly identified."

SilverTips for SUCCESS

⭐ SilverTips for REVIEW

Review what you've learned. Use the text to help you.

Define key terms

artificial intelligence (AI)　　fact-check
data　　feedback
deep learning

Check for understanding

What is a deepfake?

Why are deepfakes a problem?

What can people do about deepfakes?

Think deeper

Why are some deepfakes dangerous? What are some ways to tell if an image or video is a deepfake?

SilverTips on TEST-TAKING

- **Make a study plan.** Ask your teacher what the test is going to cover. Then, set aside time to study a little bit every day.

- **Read all the questions carefully.** Be sure you know what is being asked.

- **Skip any questions** you don't know how to answer right away. Mark them and come back later if you have time.

Glossary

artificial intelligence (AI) computer software that can act in a way similar to human intelligence

audio related to sound

celebrities famous people

content material or information presented, such as a photo or video

data information

deep learning a kind of AI that teaches itself using a large amount of content

fact-check to make sure information or content is true and real

feedback providing information on what has happened in the past to improve for the future

generator a computer program that uses data to make new content

robocall a prerecorded phone call that goes out to many people

Read More

Gregory, Josh. *The Trouble with Deepfakes (The AI Revolution).* Ann Arbor, MI: Cherry Lake Publishing, 2024.

Kuehl, Ashley. *Artificial Intelligence (In the News: Need to Know).* Minneapolis: Bearport Publishing, 2025.

Simons, Lisa M. Bolt. *Super Surprising Trivia about Artificial Intelligence (Super Surprising Trivia You Can't Resist).* North Mankato, MN: Capstone Press, 2024.

Learn More Online

1. Go to **FactSurfer.com** or scan the QR code below.
2. Enter "**Deepfakes**" into the search box.
3. Click on the cover of this book to see a list of websites.

Index

Biden, President Joe 18, 28

celebrities 4

data 10

deep learning 10

fact-check 20

feedback 12

generators 10, 12

governments 18, 22

images 6, 9–10, 12, 22

laws 22

music 24

Russia 18

Ukraine 18–19

videos 4, 6, 8, 12, 14, 18, 28

About the Author

Ashley Kuehl is an editor and writer specializing in nonfiction for young people. She lives in Minneapolis, MN.